WORD FOR WORD

OTHER WORD WORKS ANTHOLOGIES:

Cabin Fever: Poets at Joaquin Miller's Cabin
Jacklyn Potter, Dwaine Reeves, Gary Stein, eds.

Cool Fire
Christopher Bursk, ed.

Whose Woods These Are
Karren L. Alenier, ed.

Winners: A Retrospective of the Washington Prize
Karren L. Alenier, Hilary Tham, Miles David Moore, eds.

WORD
FOR
WORD

NANCY WHITE, EDITOR

WITH POEMS BY

Karren Alenier, Nathalie Anderson, Michael Atkinson,
Jennifer Barber, Molly Bashaw, J.H. Beall, Mel Belin, Carrie Bennett,
Peter Blair, John Bradley, Doris Brody, Sarah Browning, Christopher Bursk,
Richard Carr, Grace Cavalieri, Cheryl Clarke, Shirley Cochrane, Christopher Conlon,
Jamison Crabtree, Donna Denizé, W. Perry Epes, B. K. Fischer, Bernadette Geyer,
Barbara Goldberg, Barbara G. S. Hagerty, Linda Lee Harper, James Hopkins,
Brandon Johnson, Ann Rae Jonas, Paul Jones, Frannie Lindsay, Richard Lyons,
Elaine Magarrell, Fred Marchant, Marilyn McCabe, Judith McCombs, James McEuen,
Ron Mohring, Barbara Moore, Miles David Moore, Kathi Morrison-Taylor,
Ayaz Pirani, W.T. Pfefferle, Tera Vale Ragan, Brad Richard, Jay Rogoff,
Robert Sargeant, Prartho Sereno, Lisa Sewell, Michael Shaffner,
Enid Shomer, John Surowiecki, Maria Terrone,
Hilary Tham, Barbara Ungar, Jonathan Vaile,
Miles Waggener, Edward Weismiller,
Rosemary Winslow, Mike White,
Nancy White, Michele Wolf,
& Joseph Zealberg

Celebrating 40 Years of Publishing
THE WORD WORKS
WASHINGTON, D.C.

Cover Design: Susan Pearce Design
Cover Art: Matthew Weinstein

Library of Congress Control Number: 2016903359
International Standard Book Number: 978-0-915380-97-8

for our authors
who inspire
and our volunteers
who make books happen

CONTENTS

three: inside the writer

WHY THE BLANK PAGES?

An Introduction

This anthology celebrates over 40 years of publishing great poems at The Word Works, a tribute to our authors' talents and to the zeal and hardiness of the many staffers who have kept the press thriving over the years. It also honors our readers, without whom we would not exist. For them, for you, we chose each poem as an invitation to become part of the book.

Each poem selected burns bright, in and of itself, but we hope it will also spark a poet's response. The brief writing prompt that follows each poem asks you to try something similar on the blank page that awaits. To our authors whose longer poems I have excerpted, my apologies; in each case, I wanted to keep the poem on a single page, leaving the opposite page untouched, for the reader's own writing. Over the years, my students have read various of these poems and have tried these prompts, and it's no surprise that each poet has returned with something unique to voice. May the same be true for you.

Like any of life's enlightening forces, the power of a writing prompt lies mostly in the fact that it comes from outside yet connects with and startles out something from within. A good prompt is re-useable and flexible, moving beyond constraints of time, culture, style, voice, form. A good prompt will cause each writer to generate something true from a new slant, entirely distinct from examples or teachers. It should provide the writer with a sense that they're standing in a new spot, looking out a new window.

The suggestions here begin with the poet's most basic elements of craft, those that can transcend eras and styles. Then the prompts move gradually through the subject of language to the matter of being human, bridging in the last section to ways each poet can write from personal experience.

If your resulting poem gallops off in a direction that doesn't resemble the "example" poem and doesn't seem to result from the prompt, that is not a problem but a fresh piece of luck. In the big picture, the point of a prompt is to hop us onto the empty page, out of self-consciousness and into focus. Period. I have kept the prompts as brief as I can, assuming that either you have enough gumption as a writer to run with it, or that you are in a class or group setting where your facilitator will provide some additional guidance or suggestions if you get stuck.

We hope each poem in this collection gives new permission, invites play, and shows something about how poetry is in constant evolution, in every tribe. What we all share is that love of the word, its flavor, the taste of it in our ears, its texture on the tongue. Please savor and enjoy these marvelous poems, and join us here in creating a treasury of words that matter.

THE REMINDER

by Paul Jones
from *The End of the Hand*

the splinter in the knuckle of my right middle finger
surfaces daily; i squeeze the blister
and pus, the ocean for this perverse diver,
oozes out. for three days now i have worked at it
after the first half came up with a will.

it is birch i think.
it is a prick in my sense when i pick up tools.
it is no doubt infected. i have stuck needles, an old
hat pin, forks, knives, spoons, garden hoes down there
to work it up, but like a man becoming a frog
it is caught between elements.

Any writer will tell you: never underestimate the power of detail. One detail can steady us in a sea of abstractions, can make the huge seem graspable, can create a link between the reader and even the most remote of characters or situations. Write about the smallest detail you can clearly imagine.

THE SYNTAX OF THE BARN

by Molly Bashaw
from *The Whole Field Still Moving Inside It*

Held in place by the two pigs
strung up inside it, opened, emptied, intestines
on the floor.

The ninety-degree angles softened
by spider webs.

Holes in the rafters filled with swallows.

If the chickens got up from their eggs
too early, I knew it would disappear.

All summer, sleeping with cats in nests.
The dream in my father's voice

a part of the shape of the dust and dripping blood,
the floorboards' nails worn shiny.

The grain held the barn here. Pig slop and water
frozen in the tubs; each birthing ewe,
each testicle held the barn here.

The animals were a wall,
the voice was a wall,
the animals were a wall,
the voice was a wall.

On the roof
we ate new carrots from a bucket,

rolling the stubs up to the peak
to see if they would make it.

Think of a particular place (or time). Let your mind pick out the ugliest or least poetic details in that scene and start your poem there. Keeping all the details real, see how lyrical and complete you can become in your depiction.

TROPICAL DRINK

by Michele Wolf
from *Immersion*

It was frothy. It was silken.
It was icy on the tongue—fresh coconut
Milk, fresh pineapple juice, and the Appleton's.
We sipped one apiece on the terrace overlooking
The peaked gazebo cresting the dock and the glinty
Turquoise waters of our crescent beach, while a big-eyed
Doctor bird—a shimmering long-tailed hummingbird—
Hovered like a miniature copter in front of a blood-red
Hibiscus. When we rocked in the hammock,
The only sound we could hear was the breeze
Fanning the palm fronds. In the pool, on a pair of rafts,
As we closed our eyes in the late-day sun, the whole of our
World turned turquoise, hoisting us, floating us along.
We never drifted far, tethered by the length of your arm,
Of mine, by the buoy of our two hands joined.
And we knew we had tasted the edge of something sweet.

Wolf's poem begins by describing a "mouth experience" but expands from there and tells a story. Pick one strong sensory experience, try to describe it, and then tell the story that blooms out of that moment, fictional or real.

CERTAINLY

by Brandon Johnson
from *Love's Skin*

did they sit on the couch distant as the plush arms allowed
did they avert their eyes like drunks ignoring a whiskey shot
did they see their desire dancing on the cocktail table
did they pretend nothing was between them but air
did she have to look so good

did more than the room's hum raise the hair on their arms
did they get hotter than the clanging radiator in the corner
did more than the window light drip from their faces
did nobody say a word as an hour come and gone
did he have to feel so needy

did Luella serve nothing to avoid accusation
did Brook plan to die of thirst before giving her a chance
did her standing by the open door invite him to leave
did the door's click sound like a period

Using repetition, tap right into to the incantatory roots of our species' love affair with language. For greater flexibility, pick a simple word or phrase as your touchstone. One way to work with repetition is to write a poem entirely comprised of questions. This will insidiously invade your reader's mind, since we can't resist reaching for answers once we hear a question.

HOW TO OBTAIN   [excerpt]

by **Grace Cavalieri**
from *Creature Comforts*

It'll happen when you least expect it
Turning on its socket toward you
On its edge through air to meet you
Gleaming, when you least think it will happen
When you are lifting your leg like a
Stripper, the stocking shining and bright
Something will come your way—right then
When the priest puts a small sun on your tongue
When it is a high holiday
When the chicken is cut in half
And a green wilderness pops out...
It'll come to you the way the songs we sing ourselves
Humming under our breath, always tell the truth
When the moon goes down
When you're playing crazy eights
When you're telling a friend what you think
Or at the moment right before you call out the police
Or before your worst fear attacks you, working
Its buttocks like a brown horse...
The payoff will come to you saying
Something that cannot be learned
Quick as a twig
Crisp as a two-dollar bill in the jewelry box
Shot through the heart with self knowledge
Before you can go Bobolink, Yellow Warbler
Violet green swallow, you will know it
You always knew it
The inside person and the outside person
Become the same
Like an immigrant traveling wrinkled and free
You will show them what you need
And tell them what you want
And of dying you will say
"Is this all there is to it"
You'll have known it all the time.

Repetition can be syncopated so that it doesn't become predictable. Write a poem where the repetition evolves, continually shifting the repeating word(s) and the grammatical location of the repeating element(s).

ODE TO THAT WOMAN
DRIVING BY IN THE PINTO   [excerpt]

by Jonathan Vaile
from *Blue Cowboy*

Daddy maybe that lady
　　with the wattage blows static
　　　　but I bet you those

oversized woofers
　　are whomping, ripping and throbbing
　　　　spitting and coughing great

googlymoogly if I could be
　　romping with her in that
　　　　hatchback, I'd turn

up her treble, take on
　　her trouble, kick out her sunroof
　　　　and never look back—goddess

of groove if you hitch
　　your hips and permit
　　　　me the pleasure of peeling

your panties, in the whirling
　　conversation of our first ever
　　　　evening we'll eat each other's

everything everywhere
　　　　　　glistening

No poet ignores the sounds of the words. It's part of our job: to hear and to shape the music of the words, to orchestrate the reader's experience. Write a poem in which you are dancing with sound. Let sound guide you more than the meaning of the words. See where they will take you.

SOURCE

by Jennifer Barber
from *Works on Paper*

The sound of rain arriving before it arrives
has no sound to speak of, but it does

say something to the leaves, something the leaves
know how to take; they're leaning toward

the place where the rain is about to begin,
drawing nearer together but widening

the surface of their urgency, their need
to register each shifting of the air.

The sky darkens; the leaves have darkened too.
The waiting is hard to bear, resembling

other kinds of waiting, waiting to hear
in a waiting room, in the afternoon,

in the moments that seem to move apart
before they become whatever's to come.

Write for as long as you can about the quietest sound you can conjure clearly in your mind.

EVE'S GARDEN [excerpt]

by Nancy White
from *Sun, Moon, Salt*

1. Vulva

How like a coconut: cuppable,
shaggy, and milky-sweet
within. A soft sly sneaker, or
it's a big baby buggy! On fat
silver springs it rolls
through the sun. It is the hairy hill
where Milton's Eve reclines, resting
as if on a jelly
donut, white sugar powdering
her thighs, and she sighs, she rocks
and rises on her powder puff.

2. Clitoris

This pheasant's heart
beats in its feathered nest.
Lucifer's face alight between black
burlap wings, glossy and salt
as an olive. The whetstone
her hands return to. Oh, ship's
biscuit! The roan bronc who's already bucking
in the chute. Pineapple:
its tart cantankerous meat.

3. Labia minora

Down the center, little rooster wattles,
pressed like moist hands palm to palm,
these elephant ears hide-tough but
delicate as sea-monkeys that came
dry and dead in the mail
but–JUST ADD WATER!–squirmed
to life under the lens. Pink tippling
chimneys, iris edges plump as snails
dizzy in their shells. They're like some lace
of the sea, sheltered and spongy as chanterelles.

Poets *think* in metaphor. No matter how literal a poem is, it ends up working as a metaphor in spite of itself. Pick something specific (a body part, tool, common emotion, moment) and write a poem containing a long list of metaphors for it. Don't stop too soon.

AFTERIMAGE

by J. H. Beall
from *Hickey, the Days*

This sadness stains me
as iodine stains my skin
deep purple; or, if I rub it
quick enough, most swirling down
the coriolis of the sink
like purple clouds,
then yellow, stains me yellow,
a faint residue on my skin
indistinguishable
from an old bruise.

I would have looked longer
if I could. The red sun, quilted
through black trees, hung there
for an instant. As I look away
the disc remains,
floats before me, changing colors,
growing smaller with the night.

When I have touched you
the memory holds my skin
for hours. The smells
that have worked themselves
into pores come out slowly,
launch themselves into air that
surrounds me, that
touches as I turn,
asks the dim brain
to bring you there.

I pass other women.
The afterimage of your face
blinks on their faces
like the sun.

Present a metaphor and then expand upon it. Beall weaves between the bruise/iodine metaphor from the first stanza and another, involving color—the sun's afterimage. Try your hand at extended metaphor. Spin image (and thus meaning) out of the comparison for as long as you can.

PASSING OUT

by Karren L. Alenier
from *Wandering on the Outside*

His whole life
he knew about
emptiness.
He was an
expert
empty pockets
      stomachs
holes in his shoes.
He spent his time
looking for work
ditch digging
donut making
making holes in his
shoes he understood
he was an expert in
living without
the missing chunks.
Yesterday the state lottery
gave him a million bucks
an exchange for
all his expertise.
His mind fell
black with joy
like his body
he didn't even wonder
what his shoes
could hold.

Write a poem that only uses a very few words per line. Ask yourself to make sure that at least one word per line is interesting.

WHY BALL PLAYERS SPIT SO MUCH

by Jay Rogoff
from *The Cutoff*

On the close-up instant
    replay super
        slo
        mo:
                nicotiana—
Red Man or Beech Nut
                chewed judiciously
        into a rich liquor
                lusciously
launched
    in an upward arc
        through the brilliant lit
    dark
                rising to apogee
                    but failing
                        to attain full
                escape velocity
                    then falling
                        in its fall
                    trailing
                        a tail
                a brown comet
        dark in the lit dark
wrenched
cursed
    earthward
            to the end
                of its career
                    a fall
                    like a black angel
                        a jet of black semen
                    with a dream
                        fertile
                as air
                with a splatter
            to land
        hard
in dust.

Write a poem whose "path" down the pages echoes what is happening inside the poem.

SLEEPERS III

by **Miles Waggener**
from *Phoenix Suites*

On pitched roofs, winter's weight between bricks, sunset leaves gilded
wisps, half the sky a storm, the week's only light—it seems so

late and halved in the day the visible holds weather that
might only happen to others, never here above yards,

frozen distances unraveling at the skirts of trees
we know are hiding rooms, what some

keeper left, never us we think, a
wind's note working thin

walls, many reed
instruments—

cells where
once bees
were
kept.

Line length is another driving force of every poem's dynamics. Write a poem which builds
from short lines to long or, as in "Sleepers III," from long lines to short.

CHASM

by Rosemary Winslow
from *Green Bodies*

what   *memory*   *is this?*

                                                              Gripped

wrist in her father's hand   her socked feet   red   iced

land of snow

                kitchen lights

                               black gape

                                      plunging

remember   *Remember!*

coming at her   red in the face father

                                  And far far

away mother   across across across across

    small shoes   shiny black   gripped in her hand

White space is another way poets manipulate the impact of the words on the page. Write a poem where an unusual amount of or unexpected appearance of white space guides the pace and/or flavor of how the reader (and, first, the writer) will experience the language.

BIOGRAPHY OF WATER

by Carrie Bennett
from *biography of water*

[excerpt]

against the sky water against a noise like prayer a hymnal already
against the oddness   the captured moment
                                and the disappearance

of a filled hand :
                        (lake loon birch tree

two figures make
            a record   among the fallen leaves are
everywhere

Punctuation is another element of writing to experiment with. Write a poem that does not use punctuation, or uses it "incorrectly." See how far you can push your reader and play with the many possible ways to combine lack of punctuation with other ways we steer our readers: line breaks, white space...

O

by Mike White
from *How to Make a Bird
with Two Hands*

begins the morning and
I have only
to wonder at this egg

white and cold
in the restful bowl of
my hand

Poets can't resist writing about writing. Sometimes amusing, sometimes profound, and even though the subject can be self-referential, it always leads out again, to the world it started out trying to name in the first place. Write your own poem about one letter of the alphabet. Write from that letter's point of view? Send the letter on a quest or a vacation? Show how it would break out of jail?

SPELL

by Prartho Sereno
from *Call from Paris*

Before the alphabet was snatched up
by the mind, it belonged to the body.
Consonants huddled in the crooks of
elbow, ankle, and knee, where they thrived
on gossip and potluck dinners,
built cities with jazz clubs and intricate
webs of phone-line and highway.

But the vowels, moon-driven and drunk
on the sound of their own voices,
lived alone in the hollows and caves.

O, the Emperor of Solitude,
built his hut in the dome of the belly.
With wingspans and vision of an eagle,
I made his nest in the brows.
U, the hermit thrush, hid her rubies
in the isthmus of the throat. And the lioness
E staked claims on the mouth,
raising her cubs on intermittent light.

But it was *A*, wild and lovely,
who holed up in the heart.
Caught in the spell of *ah*...
in the ah of awaiting, or awkward
and aflame. In the nearly inaudible *ah*
of being folded into the arms
of the lover without a face.

Write a poem about the secret lives of a group of letters: what they do, think, sing, eat, drink, plot, harvest, dream... And what's going on between them?

O · ko [o-ko]

by Tera Vale Ragan
from *Reading the Ground*

—*noun*, plural **oči** [**oh-chee**]

1.   the organ of sight, in vertebrates typically one
of a pair of spherical bodies
contained in an orbit of the skull:

> Years after, she cries to her son, revealing
> the secret, how her brother Stephan died
> at her feet, stabbed in the **oko** with an ice pick
> by a jealous wedding guest. When the murderer
> was later found blinded by thorns, the police
> came to arrest her new husband, charged
> with the maiming, and put him in prison
> for the first year of their marriage.

2.   this organ with respect to the color of the iris:

> They said that her **oči** matched the color
> of distant waters, perhaps found farther
> than the Tatras or Vltava, a deeper blue
> than the three rivers. It is the blue of another
> world, time or love.

Pick a word (in English or in another language) and write up a detailed imaginary definition, then conjure up the wild example sentences that accompany the word, as if in a dictionary.

MO' BAD NAMES FOR WOMEN

by Barbara Ungar
from *Charlotte Brontë, You Ruined My Life*

It all began when Keva brought in her word
du jour: "harpy: a predatory monster
in classical mythology
having a woman's head
and the body and claws of a vulture;
an instrument of divine vengeance;
a shrewish or depraved woman."
Shrew begat virago, harridan,
bitch, cunt, ballbuster, and pigeon.

Synonyms for "whore" abound:
ho hooker harlot streetwalker slapper
prostitute concubine courtesan
slut tramp wench trull skank trick
cocktease siren trollop strumpet
Scarlet woman Jezebel vixen
nympho and her antonyms
frigid ice queen. Under "cow"

and "dog" came old-fashioned plain Jane,
wallflower, horseface, butch, scag,
busted, broke, slam-pig, fugly,
butterface (everything looks good but...)
Monet (looks good from far away but...)
and chickenhead (gives head a lot,
leading back to category two, ho).
So we found women get put down
for three things mainly: sexuality (ho),
aggression (bitch) and looks (cow).
Later I realized we'd left out bimbo,
to which Keva added twat.

Pick a word for which there are many synonyms, and spend a while collecting all the synonyms
you can think of. Then write a poem that weaves them all together.

A FEW THINGS YOU SHOULD
KNOW ABOUT ROBERTO   [excerpt]

by John Bradley
from *Love-in-Idleness: The
Poetry of Roberto Zingarello*

Roberto means, Hey you!
And, Everybody, shut up.
And, THIS DOOR IS A PUBLIC EXIT.
And, Poverty is the smell of the death of six o'clock.
And, In your cranium's darkness, the coconut
white of a cactus flower.

Roberto means, The milkweed down by the pumphouse.
And, I don't know, comrades.
I just don't know.
And, sometimes, Scram.
Roberto means, My mother slept with a crucifix
beneath her pillow, when she was pregnant,
so her son would be strong.
And, Love is not enough.
Nothing is ever enough.

Roberto means, I'm sick to death
of so much Roberto.
And, I want to be hemlock
so you can, finally, sleep.
But mostly it means, My mother
had one good thing happen to her
during this life, and it had to be
me, it had to be me.

Write a poem about your name (first, last, middle, nick...whatever you prefer) in which you make up a series of unexpected definitions for that name.

ATTAR OF VIOLETS & LONELINESS

by Richard Lyons
from *Fleur Carnivore*

Things are growing, but are not collective yet.
        A shadow bank has shifted like a dirigible

dropping water balloons of moisture, small collected lakes.
        When the sun returns,

thoughts will trellis whatever can gather itself up into the air.
        Then the day will reconsider things

the way a riding mower floats above swaths of earth
        so that the world, for a while,

seems an extension of our effort, a product of what we say.
        Drop cloths will float down over roses

and gutters will channel the downpours
        into some reservoir of waiting insatiable gravel,

some heavenly groundwater, attar of violet.
        And this is where it will have to stay,

this grievous joy, away from us who give it away
        with every little whispering mouth.

Pick two words (or terms, possibly containing more than one word, such as "Empire State Building" or "déjà vu") that, to you, feel unmatching, disparate, that will create a strange juxtaposition. Using this oddball combination as a title, write the poem that leads up to or stems from it.

EQUIVALENCIES

by Judith McCombs
from *Habit of Fire*

The fear of not writing, of having no words,

is the muscles not working, the pack top-heavy,
the hard slime on ledges where the ankle gives way,

is the sledge hammer current at the bottom of
waves coming too fast and the swimmer unable,

is the baby hung up in the birth canal,
the contractions building but its heartbeat stalls,

is the hemorrhage of vision with nothing made
yours, is the flicker of brainwaves in the same stuck
dream.

The writing is easy, the having is easy,

is the meadows opening, is the blessed deep
breath in the mouth of the runner, is the long
easy strides

riding and passing the crests of the earth,
is the surge of delivery, the new being riding

the pulsing red channel, is the mountains
riding the slower upheavals of strata and drift,

is the white surge riding the hull of the
seed as it breaks into life, the shapes
spilling over

and the words coming through, the deep dream
opening and the words coming true, the words
                    coming through.

Now use metaphor to portray first *not speaking* (or writing) and then its opposite. You might compare what it's like when the writing get "stuck" versus when it really takes off, or conjure some other kind of contrast between silence and sound.

FANTASIA ON A SMALL SKETCHBOX   by Brad Richard
from *Motion Studies*

SKETCH = BOX

Touch my broken story: brackets to slats grooved to hold boards
to hold pigment, river to rock to hold warm to cold, then to now.
Holding open. Holding shut. Held whole, a wooden book telling
water telling boy. Broken still to tell bracket to slat to river to nude to
hold.

PALETTESCAPE

Stroke and stir. Suppose green before anywhere grown. Repose of no
body, white all morning is no event but what. Is red sun black memory.
Is a whetting. My stroke and what stir.

FIGURE

To be is yet to be mastered.

LANDSKETCH

My planes are all one. What is solid is fixed flow. Gray-violet disposes
sky to think meadow to forest to rock, think flesh yet untold. Green
strokes a grassbank where my stream will away. Petals kindle out of
shadow. Round flat flames. Or. And. Sentence for now sentience.

RE: FIGURE

Rose-streaked peach and shadow-belly boy, impasto impostor. Butter-
lick and sunburn neck, no friends but green and blue. Such thick
nothings. Still touching true.

PALETTESCAPE (INVERTED)

Green sets red to fall. No sky for my yellow star. Smear me lead and
lampblack. Scar and no anthem.

BOX = X

Touch shuts my summer scene.

Pick an object or a moment and try to write imagistically about it instead of "normally,"
narratively, even grammatically. Loosen up the way you use nouns, verbs, diction, syntax.

WITHOUT WARNING

by Bernadette Geyer
from *The Scabbard of Her Throat*

No one ever warns how low
clouds can bend to lap the bay
with thirsty, gossamer tongues.

Or how life is consistently reduced
to forms of water, returning to puddles
and tears, rivers and sweat.

They don't mention how quickly
a storm can gather and cross the bay
in the rushed flight of wings and sails.

Or that life can end like this:
the fishy smell of the shore builds
and sours in your stomach, the language

of the living replaced by swish and thrum.

The negative puts a funny topspin on what the mind does with language. The mind perceives the negated element and removes it at the same time, so it is both *there*...and *not there*. Write a poem about what you can't write a poem about, "Don't write about..." Or speak the things we don't speak of: "No one ever tells you..." Or any variation. "I never dream about..." See where it takes you.

FIVE WAYS TO CHOOSE WINGS

by Doris Brody
from *Judging the Distance*

I

Blue is my favorite since
there is no blue, only
a way of seeing blue
that can look black or gray
depending on the light
and where you stand.

II

Music flies without theology.
The wings of metaphor are limited
by very little, but may not support you far.
Sleep flies in owlish silence from a tube.
Fear whines on hawkwings through the air.

III

Feathers are not strong enough
to lift us from the ground.
Metal, paper, plastic, wood,
are what the realists choose.
These can then be crafted
in so very many ways.

IV

The dog reads my pant legs.
Satisfied, he smiles
and settles down.
I don't know
where they've taken him
and can't go there.

V

If you have no cuts, they say,
you can taste, and even drink,
the strongest cobra venom. But
take care,
a drop directly
in the bloodstream kills.

Writing in sections can loosen up your way of making connections. Pick a strange or a vague
title and try it. Let each section head in a new direction...and you may surprise yourself.

JOKE

by Sarah Browning
from *Whiskey in the Garden of Eden*

That the first sin was eating
is funny like ha ha
My sister Eve puts the puffpastry
chocolateéclairmintchipicecream apple
in her mouth
and the world ends
Come on—it's too funny

That's it, isn't it?
You bit that ricekrispies
treatbananacreampie
MarsBar apple and it's all over—like, there's no
good in you etc You're not worthy
to gather up crumbs under the table blah blah blah

Appley temptation:
long branches of baklavaandwhitecake—you got it—
hang all about you ha ha ha

Pick something that everyone else is serious about and write the poem where you convince us that really it's a hilarious topic. Browning shows how funny this Bible story really is, for instance.

DEATH

[exerpt]

by Ron Mohring
from *Survivable World*

Arrives at the party late,
of course. His potential partners scatter
like bowling pins. He wants
to ditch the sickle and hood. He hates
wearing black, is certain yellow would flatter
his tone. If he could dance

just once, he'd be the life
of the party. Death hulks behind
a potted palm, jiggles
the ice in his drink, bored past belief.
They always act surprised to find
him here. How dull. He wiggles

a creaky shoulder, taps
his toes. They rattle loose in his shoe
like dice in a cup. Some nights
it's easy: a guest will just collapse
with fear. Sometimes he has to do
the work. Of course he's right

every time; who could deny
that when you're dead, you're dead? Death peeks
at his watch: it must have quit.

...

Pick a figure from mythology (Cupid, Fionn, Satan, Ananzi, Athena, etc.) or from our modern pantheon of magical figures (the tooth fairy, Mr. Clean, etc.) and show them in a different story or context.

MS. MUFFET

by M. A. Schaffner
from *The Good Opinion of
Squirrels*

The spider was nowhere near when you jumped. It had no intentions.
In fact it saw nothing before you moved but eight sets of angled
constructions.

It felt nothing, being preoccupied with colors and the hum
of the wind on its fingered filaments,
which you shredded, and to which it will come

again and again for careful repairs still oblivious to the sight
of the chair, the owers, the birds, the cat, or your hands shivering in the
sunlight.

Think of poems or songs in which the speaker or main character is in distress, and choose one
that others will recognize. Then write a poem that talks to that character; calm them, inspire
them, give them to will to fight—whatever it is they need to get back on track.

PERSEVERATION

by Marilyn McCabe
from Perpetual Motion

I'm walking downtown under the ghost of a half moon in the day sky
and think, I'm on a planet circled by a moon surrounded
by other planets circled by other moons in a galaxy circling something
and surrounded by other galaxies circling, and I'm dizzy from it,
and wonder why we developed the consciousness to ask why
we developed the consciousness to ask why we developed
that consciousness, and if our brain has a center whose tendency
is toward believing in a higher power does that disprove the existence of God,
or prove it? So I get an ice cream cone, and why not,
and carefully lick around the edges, a great tongue moon
lapping the ice cream planet, a great God tongue forming the ice cream mind,
like a thought moving around and around making sure nothing
drips out of the cosmic cone and down the cosmic arm
to fall on the pavement like the ghost of a half moon in the day sky.

Write a poem where you think about thinking...dream about dreaming...have feelings about feelings...and see what kind of circles these ponderings can help you create. McCabe creates some marvelously curved meanderings in this poem which wonders about wondering.

ASPECTS OF A SOUTHERN STORY

by Robert Sargeant
from *Aspects of a Southern Story*

[excerpt]

I. The story as told

That this black Mississippi woman, untraveled,
standing on the beach at Biloxi, her first sight
of those rounded waters, nothing but water
to the sky's edge—
the small conservative waves curling up
to her shod feet—
and she staring quietly a long time,
and finally saying slowly,
"Ain't near as big as I thought it'd be."

Write the story of a time when, after anticipation, someone is disappointed by reality.

WOMEN BATHING AT BERGEN-BELSEN

by Enid Shomer
from *Stalking the Florida Panther*

APRIL 24, 1945

Twelve hours after the Allies arrive
there is hot water, soap. Two women bathe
in a makeshift, open-air shower while nearby
fifteen thousand are flung naked into mass graves
by captured SS guards. Clearly legs and arms
are the natural handles of corpses. The bathers,
taken late in the war, still have flesh
on their bones, still have breasts. Though nudity was
a death sentence here, they have undressed
oblivious to the soldiers and their cameras.
The corpses push through the limed earth like upended
headstones. e bathers scrub their feet, bending
in beautiful curves, mapping the contours
of the body, that kingdom to which they've returned.

Pick a significant moment in history, but focus within it on a small element, whether to create
contrast (as Shomer does here) or irony or absurdity or insight.

VAN GOGH

by Barbara Moore
from *Farewell to the Body*

We are like this, in every particular,
green trying to become blue. A man
shoveling, a man eating and weeping,
leaning forward in his chair.
The edges of his flesh curl
like a thick, private page.
It is necessary to eat and weep, because
the light uses up everything,
flying back, in a rain of mallets—
as if a man should contract a fever
which does not dispel,
maintaining itself in the charred log...
The chair gnaws a hole in the floor
with its stubby, yellow root.

*

Behind the asylum at St. Remy,
the Lord is angry. The wheatfield mounts,
boils like the molten hay of heaven,
breaks and stays.
And now my life begins, under a poultice
clapped over the left side of my face which
is green and melting. I
will rake the stubble behind this heavy house
where the windows slam open, offending me. That
bench in the corner is lonelier than Christ.

Lord, you lit these ligaments,
make me the thing of terror which you made,
phosphoring through all the layers. Watch,
I will make the sun stop on a hill, the
rock expel a tongue of cypress,
then a ruck of constellations. I,
cantering, milk of gold!
You have not seen such things.
You have never made a blue like the blue
I made in the lake behind the fields at St. Remy.

Choose a famous person who intrigues you. Write the monologue that expresses that
person's essence.

THE MEN IN MARGE'S LIFE

by John Surowiecki
from *The Hat City After Men Stopped Wearing Hats*

One liked her kamikazes and mojitos
and surprised her with nighties and mules.
One, an electrician, wound her life around his
as he would wire around his arm. One
had one nipple. One thumbed the moon

out of the sky as if it were a lozenge in a silver
wrapper and placed it at her feet. One provided
examples but never explanations as to why love
becomes unborn in a misappropriation of time.

One let her basil go to seed and her peonies
go flowerless; and in a snapshot she took,
one is his own ghost, double-exposed and half
cigarette smoke, oating above the first
unshoveled morning of our last hard winter.

Create a portrait gallery by choosing a group of people and describing each individual with a detail or two in rapid succession, as Surowiecki does. You can generalize large (Red Sox fans, professors, girls who eat scrapple) or personalize it more (my five first friends, we who failed calculus, my wife's weird cousins...etc.).

EIGHT FEARS   [excerpt]

by Nathalie F. Anderson
from *Following Fred Astaire*

1.   Aulophobia
          Fear of Flutes

Right or wrong. Three silver birches
bar the window. So nearly straight.
Wind thin as a shiv. Desperate
teeth behind their silver bar.

Grasp and twist. Silver splits, shreds, flays.
Diminuendo. Lips blister,
stops spew hoarse waxy curds. Spiked through,
the rag's scummy. Trill. Tremolo.

Keen, you were keen. Tense. Again tense.
Keep it shrill. Knife at the teeth, wind
like a shiv. Upright, unfallen.
Silver birch. Silver blade. Spike. Bleb.

Invent a fear and give it a name, or go online and research the multitudes of phobias out there until you find one you have never heard of before. Then write a poem full of all the things that might set off that fear in a person and/or explore how that fear was created in the first place.

QUESTIONS TO BE ASKED OF
A FULLY PROGRAMMED COMPUTER

by Edward Weismiller
from *The Branch of Fire*

What is the water
in whose bright surface
remaining swimmers
struggle for joy?

How did the walker
dark and selfless
turn, those summers
ago, into air?

Sleeper and waker,
whose is the silence
in which earth stammers
Let — be — ?

Taker of fire, where?

Weismiller imagines asking non-logical questions of a computer so completely programmed that it could understand everything. Create your own list of impossibly unanswerable questions, perhaps the ones that will cause the ultimate mainframe to crash.

WEEK 4 (FABRICATION)

by B. K. Fischer
from *St. Rage's Vault*

We made her the usual way,
with spools and cocoons and a wisp
of frayed thread. That business

about the woof took time.
We spun her up and wondered

whose side is she on, anyway?
Whose eyes and the slouch
of whose shoulders? We loomed

over her day and night, sometimes
offering the wrong thing.

We gave her a name,
a counterpane and a slap,
sang songs about a larva

that were both kind and true.
She wriggled right out

of the swaddling as soon as
we got the story going.

Imagine you can invent a person. (If you are a parent, you may already have done this.) Write
the poem in which you put this person together and make life happen.

THE IMMACULATE

by Christoper Conlon
from *Mary Falls: Requiem for Mrs. Surratt*

They speak English, these deep-throated
creatures, these men; they walk upright
on two legs, laugh and sing, exhibit
table manners (some of them) and
they're handsome (some of them): her son
John, or the occasional gray-suited officer
who passes through the tavern for a whiskey
or a meal. Once as a girl she watched
a farmer swinging a pickax onto a stump,
a man who wore no shirt at all, whose chest
gleamed luminously in the summer sun,
and she'd nearly fallen, breathless with
this vision of man's perfection, and God's.
Yet she finds something inescapably
foreign about them, all of them, as if they had
descended from some other world to dazzle,
to enchant, to abuse, to kill, but never
just to live, never simply to be, not born
of woman at all—or rather, not of man:
unfathered, adrift in their individual
loveless universes, each one distant, alone,
immaculate in his beauty and violence, poised
to engulf her in his icy, alienated embrace.

Write about a group or category of people who feel alien to you. In writing, try to draw closer
to understanding or appreciating something about this "Other."

BINGES [excerpt]

by Linda Lee Harper
from *Toward Desire*

Hiding in the woods
after Saturday night binges
is Effie's way
of aggravating the shit
out of her old man.
He'll cut willow to whip
the orneriness out of her
and like a runaway cat
who vaguely remembers
the hand that's fed her,
she'll sneak slowly back
toward him where,
shirt off against the heat,
he stands waiting on the back porch.
He whittles on the end of the green wood
and occasionally snaps it over his head
like a jockey about to race his prize mare,
both eyeing the other,
wary and ready.

Some Sunday mornings
she knows he's thought about
tracking her. Once she found
his bootprints, clear and deep
leading to the edge of the woods.
He just called, *Effie, Effie,*
would not go in without the dogs,
and he lost them at cards.
These are facts that, like her,
sometimes get away from him.
...

Write about a relationship you have observed that disturbs you, telling a story that shows what causes your reaction. Use detail and narrative to cause the same unrest in your reader, not analysis or explanation.

LAMENT FOR THE INVISIBLE MAN

by Jamison Crabtree
from *Rel[am]ent*

Plastic bags from the piggly wiggly riffle themselves

unstuck from razor wire everyday, almost whole. And
you suspected that there were no more miracles.

Bud, I didn't understand the how of vanishing, only the need. What from

or where to is as irrelevant as your unbandaged body: it's not apparent.

You could twist the neck
of the desk lamp and it still won't notice you. I thought
(I think) I wanted that too.

I'll tell you about the end: when you died
everyone saw you again. They took photographs.

Dragged a chair up to the casket and stood on it
so they could get a good shot from above the open lid. All death is funny

like the song a piano plays
when it hits a man. Funny. Keep repeating that, repeat it
until it seems true.

Best not to let it trouble you.

And no matter what I do, what I'm saying

is that I understand what you're saying.

Pick a villain, monster, or anti-hero from popular fiction or film and write a poem addressed directly to that character.

CIVILIAN, LATE TWENTIETH CENTURY

by W. Perry Epes
from *Nothing Happened*

There's no front line, no rear.
I'll be crouched beside a pocked wall
when gusts of wind assail,
rudely refurling my umbrella,
snatching it up like a dress
above my bared head,
and there I'll be, shucked.

Write the poem that shows what it means to be vulnerable, "shucked," truly seen in your particular time and place.

CHAMPAGNE

by Richard Carr
from *Ace*

I live in a flowering meadow
there is so little for me to understand
I have tiny hands tiny feet
perfect toes the size of champagne bubbles
a wisp of spinal cord
like a candle wick in soft wax
gently shut eyes
heartbeat
heartbeat
a flowering meadow for me to understand
I kick and grasp
I suck my thumb
there is so little for me
except this my great beginning.

Write the part of your life story that comes from before you were born, using any point of view that feels right to you.

IMMIGRANT ASTRONAUT

by Ayaz Pirani
from *Happy You Are Here*

I can't get over being on Earth.
It helps that I'm with you but who knows
what you see in me
                    or place in me
each time I'm near your fragrance?

I'm getting up from this chair.
I haven't stood up from it before
but I'm standing now
and by that I mean no harm.

It's just that you've put in the hard work.
Go ahead and say the words

that you'll never hear me say
which explain my face.

My mouth is a hummingbird's lodge.
He took up residence in me
when I came to the New World. That's

when all my color flew inward
                        and I grew neutral and flagless
iridescent only on the inside.

Write about the part of yourself that feels alien to the place where you are, even if you have lived here your whole life. Shift perspective, or, if you just can't do that, picture yourself in a completely new place.

TWINZILLA DISTURBOLOGY

by Barbara G. S. Hagerty
from *Twinzilla*

Even before you majored in disturbology,
we were already *dui generis*. Though all talk
is theory, the moment's warehouse stores
swizzle sticks, quantum mechanics, Larry Levis's
Great Aunt No One. Tune an ear to the turning universe,
its valves' whoosh and fall. Doesn't everybody have
an "evil twin" who sings inside the wreck?
O, doublemint and paradox, my once lush and easy-speak,
when White Russians downed Pink Ladies in Margaritaville
and Manhattan, when we lived on Planet Ashtray.
When you were my armed and dangerous,
sound and fury, crash and burn, we shared a skin.
I'm still here with my rack and pinion, lock and load,
my alive and kicking, my warm and fuzzy.
Here, put on my robe and bunny slippers. Sleep deep.

Invent or borrow a monster or some other form of alter-ego, and write a poem to your own alter-ego, or let that monster speak to us. Hagerty puts a spin on "Godzilla" in her character "Twinzilla," a sort of anti-mom about/to whom her speaker addresses a series of poems. Once you have conjured your self-not-self, stand back and see what comes out.

THE BRAIN ON ITS OWN

by Elaine Magarell
from *Blameless Lives*

It was the brain's idea to leave
the body. Finally it could forget
the conundrum of marriage, the need
to be close and the need to be separate.
It would jet to Paris, maybe shop
for an outrageous thesis. But without
the body it could only dream of pleasure—
the brain was denied the special dispensations
of sex. Weather ceased to be an event.
How it longed for the hair's experiments.
The brain was bored. Given another
chance, it would squander every thought
on the flesh. It sought out the body,
serene in a bubble bath. The body
was stiff having danced all night
without feeling self conscious.
And it was in love with another body.

Pick one of your body parts and write the piece in which it pursues a life of its own. It doesn't have to jet off to Paris, as in Magarrell's poem, but it no longer needs the rest of you, so what does it choose to do?

SONG OF THE STOMACH [excerpt]

by Fred Marchant
from *Tipping Point*

I will rub the hair toward the center,
the way it wants to go, and I will not
deny the strange pleasure of holding myself,
of fingering the depth from the brim
to the swirl of the navel.

I will remember the word Butterball,
my detested schoolyard name.
I will remember dreading Thanksgiving,
and the ads for basted, dripping rounds of turkey.

I couldn't understand how even I in fat
could be thought to look like that.
To look like that.
I will try to remember the origin of my shames.
The quick instinct to cover, to stay underwater,
to slip unnoticed to the sexual sidelines.
I will hate every thought of Darwin.

I will remember too the miraculous onset:
not only hair below to surprise me, but the sleek
suddenness with which the child's body shed
what everyone said was baby fat. My amazement
at the way I was welcomed into the communion
of ordinary bodies. How there were girls
who didn't even know me when I was fat,
who couldn't believe me when I said I was,
or had been, and who were wide-eyed with sweetness
they had no idea they possessed.

With both hands I will hold this portion of myself
before the bright morning of the world.
I will declare it my *felix culpa*,
my fall into the fallen,
my unruly badge of imperfection,
my doorway into the world of the shunned.
I will try not to hate you.

Pick a body part you are critical of, and write about it until you feel the love, and maybe insight.

THE EXAMINED LIFE

by Maria Terrone
from *The Bodies We Were Loaned*

I'm looking to hire a private eye to spy
on myself, someone invisible equipped with a scope
and insight. I want a pro who'll
float above my shoulder, taking notes, ascribing
motives, but mostly I want an hour by hour
record of every texture, sight, and sound—the solid
facts. She wore a 30s chiffon dress and vivid
pink lipstick Saturday. She bought sunflowers
and every few hours that night her face cropped
up beside them, bothering the pane like a pebble.
I want a full report on my life without double
talk, words like 'hunger' or 'joy.' So if my diary stops
and mind shuts down, I'll have proof, delivered
daily, Here it is. She came and went. She lived.

Imagine hiring a "private eye" to scout your life. Create the point of view of someone looking in at your life from the outside, not knowing anything about you beforehand. What would they see? Let the detective/witness notice the details...including ones you don't see yourself.

ON HERITAGE NIGHT AT MY CHILDREN'S ELEMENTARY SCHOOL

by Kathi Morrison-Taylor
from *By the Nest*

I show up with brownies, nothing exotic or ethnic
or spicy, no soul food, fried rice, or plantains.
In a Betty Crocker pyramid, I display my dark, sugary fix
awkwardly, pretending a wholesome American heritage,

while inside, I am the dilute white of my father's alcoholic amnesia,
a translucent fog as homogenous as a mild cold.
I show up with brownies out of a box, whisked with oil,
eggs and water, the color of brandy in his morning coffee,

dense and slightly under-baked. I set them on a table in the gym,
wondering what others will think of me, wondering
what I think of them. In the addict's kingdom that's how you think,
sizing up others, who like you, may hear heritage and know

Jack Daniels, gin, or a six-pack could as easily appear as this array
of international casseroles. In a United Nations' stew of young families,
screw my historic English, Swedish, Scottish, French blood lines.
Our parents teach us what to do, or not to do, in my case.

Find an event in your memory that allows write about some part of your personal heritage that isn't visible to the naked eye, claiming or rejecting that element of where you come from or how you (or your family) have lived.

DON'T WANT TO GO

by Cheryl Clarke
from *By My Precise Haircut*

no farther back than
under the bed to look at moldy photo albums from the 30s
not the Gold nor Guinea Coast nor even Tulsa where
your nasty great-great-grandfather made a fortune
and lost it in that race riot.

No deed of an old maid slave mistress' whose
surname is spelled exactly like mine
or letters from a silly alcoholic birth father
or trading baseball cards with a sweet cousin half-sister.

No matricide or
murdered same-sex lover or
botched (secret) abortions
loud (secret) adoptions.

No accidental asphyxiation of a baby girl under
the drunken bodies of her loving parents.

Write about your family or cultural history, the history of a group you feel you belong to,
either as something you do or you do not want to remember or "go back into."

THE SOOTHSAYER IS SUMMONED TO INTERPRET BLANCHEFLOR'S DREAM

by Barbara Goldberg
from *Berta Broadfoot and Pepin the Short*

i. The Dream

In this dream the dreamer knows
she is dreaming. Holds a wide-
toothed comb in her hand. Soft
thump at door. Enter a bear.
She pulls comb through dark fur.
Strong odor of musk, honey,
cloves. Dreamer sings lulla,
lullaby, go to sleep my plump
sweet. Bear sucks on paw.
Paw becomes raking claw.
Tears cheek, rips right arm,
begins to gnaw at dreamer's
rib-cage. Scatters bones on floor.
Dreamer finds mirror. Torso
a carcass. Right arm dangles
from its socket. Face half-
gone. Bear sees bear. Mirror
mirror. Bear bear. Thump thump.

ii. The Interpretation

I bind phylacteries with ribbons
to my arms, with cords to my legs.
Combine letters of dreamer's name.
I climb to the rooftop, pay heed
to the direction of smoke. Examine
the excrement of a cat. Study
the sky. Make note that moon
in fourth quarter. Omen of death.
Comet appears in sign of Scorpio.
Open book at random. Scrutinize
all data. Interpretation: extreme
danger to dreamer's daughter. Long
voyage required. Dreamer pulls hair
in lamentation. There is no pleasure
to such work.

Write the two-part poem that first shows what someone dreamed, then invents a wild interpretation. Include your method of "divination," as Goldberg does, or just share the results.

THE SKIFF

by **Christopher Bursk**
from *The Way Water Rubs Stone*

Even as a small boy he was afraid
of what he imagined: sailing away from everyone
to an island that must exist
because he wanted it so badly.
He loved his family
but was convinced he'd have to leave them,
drop the centerboard, steer away
from all allegiances. He practiced
tacking into the wind,
each voyage, putting another mark behind him,
Gull's Rock, then Minot's Ledge,
then the lightship. And when there were no islands,
he let out the mainsheet on a long run
as if to sail out of Plymouth Bay
and into the infinities.
Not till he got so far out from land
he could stop believing in it,
did he reef his sail and drop overboard.
Naked, he wanted the risk
of the boat drifting away,
of there being no one to rescue him.
Arms held at his side,
legs locked at the ankles, he sank.
He made no motion to save himself
so the ocean would rush around him,
lift him up,
his face pressed into its huge, muscular shoulders.
He knew precisely when to pull away:
not till the terror was real,
not till he had to swim harder than ever before,
only just reaching the painter,
reining in the boat,
pulling himself aboard.
Lying on his back, he offered himself to the sun,
took its heat deep into his body.

Think back to something you were afraid of as a child. Write the poem in which you contend with that fear, whether or not you actually confronted it at the time—any way you want to tackle it.

ANUBIS

by James McEuen
from *Snake Country*

The sick cat has gone
off feed; the vet says nothing

to be done, which the cat
knows already, staring straight

as it does all day
into its death,

whose jackal eyes blaze back
from the ancient sands of some Egypt

where cats are gods.

Write about a time someone (human or otherwise) was dying, when one or both of you
knew it was coming.

FATSLUG IS MAAAD

by Miles David Moore
from *Rollercoaster*

those stupid people at the stupid
supermarket have a stupid
RAILING up so he can't take the
STUPID cart to the STUPID car
and has to drive around to the entrance
leaving SEVENTY-FIVE DOLLARS worth of FOOD
out unattended where some stupid WINO
can STEAL it or put his PAWS on it

and now some STUPID woman is parked
in the STUPID middle of the STUPID road
shooting the STUPID breeze with her STUPID friend
what else can Fatslug do
but L-A-Y-O-N-T-H-E-H-O-R-N

and the old man
hobbling down the sidewalk
jumps at the sound of the horn
turns around
looks at Fatslug as if he'd shot him

and slowly, slowly shakes his head.

Remember or invent a time you completely lost your temper, and have a great time telling
about it, either by making it humorous or by relishing the anger as pleasure.

WARNING IN THE MOTHER TONGUE

by Shirley Cochrane
from *Family and Other Strangers*

He may not kill you right away
or use a gun to do it. He could
live with you twenty years
then turn you out in the woods
or run you down on the highway
driving off in that car
the color of winter apples.

The men with the light-tan eyes
and mill hair are the worst—
the ones who know how to turn
you against yourself. A girl
your age needs to listen
to a wiser voice. So ask—
that is, if he allows you time.

Look back in time and ponder what you wish you had known earlier. Write the poem of advice for those who come after you, those who are younger or just haven't yet experienced what you have, creating the advice you wish you could have received in time.

SHORT BUT SWEET

by Joe Zealberg
from *Covalence*

On the morning of my circumcision
the Mohel required a magnifying glass.
Perhaps it was cold that day, frigid, sub-zero.
My parents explained, Yes, it was November, in the hills.
They remember a stag behind a hemlock, heavy with ice.
Was this an omen or a dreamed excuse?
I thought my therapist had cured this obsession.
Yet I often dream that my wife complains, says she wants sex
in the back of the car, but still expects me to drive.
Then I feel the desire to defend myself. I want to say,
in Junior High they called me King Kong, Meat Bat,
Elephant Guy in Heat. I want to brag. I want to cry.
I tell her, We can make seated love, rodeo style
in the open trunk, on top of the spare tire
and I'll still be able to reach the steering wheel.
This could be bad sleep apnea or penile friction.
In the recurring dream, she calls me Small Boy.
Runt Hose. Pencil Point Stud. Then she walks out,
smelling good. I hear the click of her red high heels
and my blood pressure seems to rise. When I wake,
I sweat and scratch at my arms. What can a guy do?
I grab a beer, then listen to Elton John's "Rocket Man,"
Tom Waits' plaintive tune "Hold On," or
"Waiting for the Miracle" by Leonard Cohen.

Select some aspect of yourself about which you feel insecure. Write the poem that liberates you from that doubt, whether through rage, compassion, or, as in Zealberg's poem, through exaggeration that creates hilarity.

OYSTER   [excerpt]

by James Hopkins
from *Eight Pale Women*

IV.

last night
i turned sailor
on a rolling deck,
was lifted and tossed
to the waiting sea.
i struck the surface
with a crack and shattered
fragments scattered
across the waves
to fall dusting, drifting
through a cobalt eye.
phosphorous ghosts
in silent descent
settled across
a lightless floor
where you waited then
on an alabaster bed
to suck me into
a slippery mantle
and roll me
slowly
to pearl.

First, think of a relationship in your life that has been difficult to put into words. Then choose a place that somehow feels similar to that relationship. Describe the place, and then address the person as if you are a part of this place together. Invent what happens here.

WEBS

by Mel Belin
from *Flesh That Was Chrysalis*

Like wisps of morning fog
not burnt off, or festive
bunting on buttonbush,
lizard's tail. An odd patchwork
of directions in these spider
webs: slanted diagonal
vertical athwart in
meadow wetlands. We, who
have been stuck, hand here,
heart there, weave our lives beside
the like of these, spinning out
the fabric too, sometimes
invisible, not sure
if any of it can be
undone. Salvador Dali—his
limp clocks folded over
branches like slices
of cheese or linen to dry—
would've loved to paint all
of this. He, who understood
the timelessness in perfervid
phenomena, would've reached
for his palette, but now
instead of blood and maggot,
the fine silken strand.

Write about a time you were stuck. Use all your poetic tools to show the place, the feeling, the causes...possibly the hint of a solution?

MRS. WEI ON THE BUS

by Hilary Tham
from *The Tao of Mrs. Wei*

found a seat, thankfully set down her bags.
Hot bodies jostled her: schoolgirls in blue,
women shoppers, salesmen, a Buddhist monk

carrying his alms pouch. A schoolgirl
near him struggled towards the exit.
She stumbled over Mrs. Wei's bags.

Mrs. Wei helped her up. "Why are you
leaving? You just got on. Are you
feeling sick?"

Eyes wide, the girl shook her head.
"No—he—the Monk touched me.
I'll catch the next bus."

Mrs. Wei rose in wrath, hissed to the girl
to watch her bags and began to bellow.
"Lecher! Animal! Reptile in saffron robe!

Secret Eater of Forbidden Meat!
Molesting young girls on buses!
I'll report you to your Abbot,

you vomit on Buddha's face!"
Eyes turned. Heads turned. In silence
he took the path that opened to the exit.

"Always carry a safety-pin," Mrs. Wei said
to the schoolgirl. "When scum like that
surfaces, stab it in the ass.

That jackal is going to be
a lizard in his next life.
May Lord Buddha have mercy on his soul!"

Write a poem about a time you stuck up for someone, or someone stuck up for you. Let your detail do the work of showing, without fanfare, that moment of heroism. If there is no such time, make one up: what should have happened.

MAP OF MY FATHER'S DEATH

by Ann Rae Jonas
from *A Diamond Is Hard but Not Tough*

The last roads he walked are pale: here legs
and mind faltered. In these buildings, they tried
to bolster a body winding down, then advised
a lowering of expectations—rising from the couch
slowly, patience with fumbling for keys. Cities
and towns have misspelled names. Foliage is
faint, the coastline blurred. This is the road
where his decline hastened. With few turns and no
intersections, it goes clear to the end of the page.

Pick a significant event from your life, and instead of telling the story, show us the map of the event.

TO THE AQUARIUM, BRIGHTON BEACH

by Donna Denizé
from *Broken like Job*

The day we went to the aquarium
we rode the train with an English woman
whose hands moved like one knitting—no needles,
no yarn, or like birds, wings pressing air,
and I asked myself, did she find what she went to see?

She was swimming in joy like the dolphins
as she shared the tale of her day, and I
kept wondering, did she find what she went
to see, she whose bags were filled with remnants,
and whose hands moved with the grace of dancers?

Write about a time you encountered a stranger in a surprisingly vivid or interesting way. It may be a portrait of the stranger, or of the moment of connection itself.

MY BAD GIRLFRIEND BLOWS HER NOSE ON MY SLEEVE

by W.T. Pfefferle
from *My Coolest Shirt*

She fake cries at Sandy Bullock movies.

She gets her hair cut in Petaluma
(where I must drive her).
She makes me pay, and stiffs them on the tip.

She wants me to buy her lip liner, eye shadow.
She scatters pages of Glamour magazine
on the kitchen table.

She wears big boots and clomps
when I want to sleep.
She makes French toast and puts raspberry jam on it.

She wants to change her name to Jasmine.
She treats me to an extra-thick milkshake
then leaves lipstick on the straw.

She pulls pages out of my notebook
and fills them with terrifying poems
she says are love poems, but are clearly not.

She kisses my neighbor under the mistletoe
with an open mouth.
When she laughs, she slugs my bad arm.

She does my crossword in pen,
spelling out names of old boyfriends,
the names of her sister's cats,

and "XOXO" when nothing else fits.

Write your own "My Bad ... (fill in the blank)" poem.

GRACE

by Frannie Lindsay
from *Mayweed*

Praise my plain young mother for leaving
her husband's bed at four in the morning
fumbling around for her bifocals
carting her stained velour slippers
down the raw-grained stairs not tying
her robe sliding her violin from between
the magazine rack and the firewood
easing past the mantelpiece scattered
with wedding portraits

praise the caked galoshes drying beside
the basement door swollen away
from its frame and the top step's narrow slat
praise her large bare feet
their tough and knotty bunions
the cool of her hand on her sheet music
praise the scotch tape on the spine
of her Bach and its weakening glue
her penciled maiden name

praise the steadfast ladderback chair
and the music stand there in the basement
the set tubs the damp socks
and undershirts draped too close
to her shoulders praise her shoulders
limber and painless for three brief hours
praise the rosin's glide down her bow
the throaty fifths the sacrament
of her tuning

praise the measure she counted aloud
and the downbeat's breath-lunge
praise her calloused and lovely fingerpads
the noteprints the sixty-watt bulb
the mud-plashed screen through which
the unsorrowing ends of the night slipped in
and although she did not ask to be touched
praise how they lifted up the brittle
ends of her perm.

Write about a quality in one of your parents that lies outside the family or his/her role in it.

LETTERS TO A YOUNG POET

by Lisa Sewell
from *Impossible Object*

Out of our arguments with ourselves, what is lost
in translation is news that stays news, a small (or large)
machine made of words that makes nothing
happen, comes nearer to vital truth than history,
and must go in fear, be as new as foam, as old
as the rock, have something in it that is barbaric,
vast and wild, a way of taking life by the throat.
And out of this turning within, out of this immersion
in your own world, as if the top of my head were taken off
for lack of what is found there or in the journal
of a sea animal living on land, wanting to fly in the sky,
in the best words, in the best order, put things before
his eyes: imaginary gardens with real toads that spring
from genuine feeling that the mind is dangerous
and my whole body so cold no fire can ever warm me—

What would you try to say to future poets about poetry? Sewell's title references Rilke's famous letters, and the poem itself alludes to the words of many others... But what do you need to say about poetry?

ABOUT THE WORD WORKS

The Word Works, a nonprofit literary organization, publishes contemporary poetry and presents public programs. As a 501(c)3 organization, The Word Works has received awards from the National Endowment for the Arts, the National Endowment for the Humanities, the D.C. Commission on the Arts & Humanities, the Witter Bynner Foundation, Poets & Writers, The Writer's Center, Bell Atlantic, the David G. Taft Foundation, and others, including many generous private patrons.

WORD WORKS BOOKS

Annik Adey-Babinski, *Okay Cool No Smoking Love Pony*
Karren L. Alenier, *Wandering on the Outside*
Karren L. Alenier & Miles David Moore, eds., *Winners: A Retrospective of the Washington Prize*
Christopher Bursk, ed., *Cool Fire*
Barbara Goldberg, *Berta Broadfoot and Pepin the Short*
Frannie Lindsay, *If Mercy*
Marilyn McCabe, *Glass Factory*
Ann Pelletier, *Letter That Never*
Ayaz Pirani, *Happy You Are Here*
W.T. Pfefferle, *My Coolest Shirt*
Jacklyn Potter, Dwaine Rieves, Gary Stein, eds., *Cabin Fever: Poets at Joaquin Miller's Cabin*
Robert Sargent, *Aspects of a Southern Story & A Woman from Memphis*
Fritz Ward, *Tsunami Diorama*
Amber West, *Hen & God*

INTERNATIONAL EDITIONS

Kajal Ahmad (Alana Marie Levinson-LaBrosse, Mewan Nahro Said So , and Darya Abdul-Karim Ali Najin, trans., with Barbara Goldberg), *Handful of Salt*
Keyne Cheshire (trans.), Murder at Jagged Rock: *A Tragedy by Sophocles*
Jean Cocteau (Mary-Sherman Willis, trans.), *Grace Notes*
Yoko Danno & James C. Hopkins, *The Blue Door*
Moshe Dor, Barbara Goldberg, Giora Leshem, eds., *The Stones Remember: Native Israeli Poets* Moshe Dor (Barbara Goldberg, trans.), *Scorched by the Sun*
Lee Sang (Myong-Hee Kim, trans.), Crow's Eye View: *The Infamy of Lee Sang, Korean Poet* Vladimir Levchev (Henry Taylor, trans.), *Black Book of the Endangered Species*

THE TENTH GATE PRIZE

Jennifer Barber, *Works on Paper*, 2015
Roger Sedarat, *Haji As Puppet: An Orientalist Burlesque*
Lisa Sewell, *Impossible Object*, 2014

THE WASHINGTON PRIZE

Nathalie Anderson, *Following Fred Astaire*, 1998
Michael Atkinson, *One Hundred Children Waiting for a Train*, 2001
Molly Bashaw, *The Whole Field Still Moving Inside It*, 2013
Carrie Bennett, *biography of water*, 2004
Peter Blair, *Last Heat*, 1999
John Bradley, *Love-in-Idleness: The Poetry of Roberto Zingarello*, 1995, 2nd edition 2014
Christopher Bursk, *The Way Water Rubs Stone*, 1988
Richard Carr, *Ace*, 2008
Jamison Crabtree, *Rel[AM]ent*, 2014
Jessica Cuello, *Hunt*
Barbara Duffey, *Simple Machines*, 2015
B. K. Fischer, *St. Rage's Vault*, 2012
Linda Lee Harper, *Toward Desire*, 1995
Ann Rae Jonas, *A Diamond Is Hard but Not Tough*, 1997
Frannie Lindsay, *Mayweed*, 2009
Richard Lyons, *Fleur Carnivore*, 2005
Elaine Magarrell, *Blameless Lives*, 1991
Fred Marchant, *Tipping Point*, 1993, 2nd edition 2013
Ron Mohring, *Survivable World*, 2003
Barbara Moore, *Farewell to the Body*, 1990
Brad Richard, *Motion Studies*, 2010
Jay Rogo , *The Cutoff*, 1994
Prartho Sereno, *Call from Paris*, 2007, 2nd edition 2013
Enid Shomer, *Stalking the Florida Panther*, 1987
John Surowiecki, *The Hat City After Men Stopped Wearing Hats*, 2006
Miles Waggener, *Phoenix Suites*, 2002
Charlotte Warren, *Gandhi's Lap*, 2000
Mike White, *How to Make a Bird with Two Hands*, 2011
Nancy White, *Sun, Moon, Salt*, 1992, 2nd edition 2010
George Young, *Spinoza's Mouse*, 1996

THE HILARY THAM CAPITAL COLLECTION

Nathalie Anderson, *Stain*

Mel Belin, *Flesh That Was Chrysalis*

Carrie Bennett, *The Landscape Is a Painted Thing*

Doris Brody, *Judging the Distance*

Sarah Browning, *Whiskey in the Garden of Eden*

Grace Cavalieri, *Pinecrest Rest Haven*

Christopher Conlon, *Gilbert and Garbo in Love* & *Mary Falls: Requiem for Mrs. Surratt* Donna

Denizé, *Broken like Job*

W. Perry Epes, *Nothing Happened*

David Eye, *Seed*

Bernadette Geyer, *The Scabbard of Her Throat*

Barbara G. S. Hagerty, *Twinzilla*

James Hopkins, *Eight Pale Women*

Brandon Johnson, *Love's Skin*

Marilyn McCabe, *Perpetual Motion*

Judith McCombs, *The Habit of Fire*

James McEwen, *Snake Country*

Miles David Moore, *The Bears of Paris* & *Rollercoaster*

Kathi Morrison-Taylor, *By the Nest*

Tera Vale Ragan, *Reading the Ground*

Michael Sha ner, *The Good Opinion of Squirrels*

Maria Terrone, *The Bodies We Were Loaned*

Hilary Tham, *Bad Names for Women* & *Counting*

Barbara Louise Ungar, *Charlotte Brontë, You Ruined My Life* & *Immortal Medusa*

Jonathan Vaile, *Blue Cowboy*

Rosemary Winslow, *Green Bodies*

Michele Wolf, *Immersion*

Joe Zealberg, *Covalence*

CPSIA information can be obtained
at www.ICGtesting.com
Printed in the USA
LVHW101548010821
694270LV00006B/439